Reptiles & Amphibians
Birth & Growth

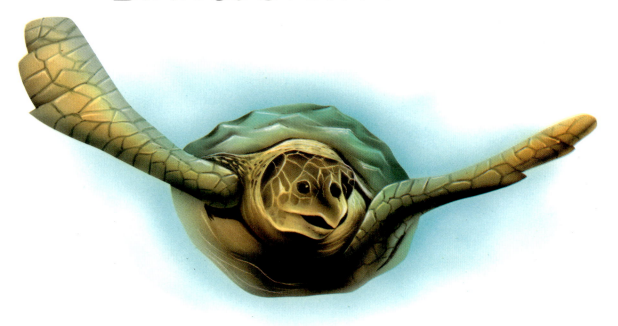

Andres Llamas Ruiz
Illustrated by Ali Garousi

Sterling Publishing Co., Inc.
New York

Library of Congress Cataloging-in-Publication Data Available

Illustrations by Ali Garousi
Text by Andres Llamas Ruiz
Translated by Natalia Tizon
Edited by Carol Townsend, Associate, Department of Herpetology
American Museum of Natural History, New York

1 3 5 7 9 10 8 6 4 2

Published by Sterling Publishing Company, Inc
387 Park Avenue South, New York, N.Y. 10016
Contains the following material originally published in Spain
by Ediciones Este, S.A.: *Nacer Y Crecer: Los Reptiles* © 1994 and
Nacer Y Crecer: Los Anfibios © 1995 by Ediciones Este, S.A.
English version and translation © 1996 by Sterling Publishing Company, Inc.
Distributed in Canada by Sterling Publishing
℅ Canadian Manda Group, One Atlantic Avenue, Suite 105
Toronto, Ontario, Canada M6K 3E7
Distributed in Great Britain and Europe by Cassell PLC
Wellington House, 125 Strand, London WC2R 0BB, England
Distributed in Australia by Capricorn Link (Australia) Pty Ltd.
P.O. Box 6651, Baulkham Hills, Business Centre, NSW 2153, Australia

Printed and bound in Spain
All rights reserved

Sterling ISBN 0-8069-6127-9

Contents

THE REPTILES	4
Finding a mate	6
Fighting for the female	8
Courtship and mating	10
Building a nest	12
Reptile eggs	14
Reptiles that do not lay eggs	16
Development inside the egg	18
Hatching	20
Protecting the babies	22
Learning to live	24
Molting	26
Escape from enemies	28
Fascinating reptiles	30
Baby reptiles	32

THE AMPHIBIANS	34
Migrating to reproduce	36
Attracting a mate	38
Courtship	40
Laying the eggs	42
Eggs with special care	44
Growing inside the egg	46
Hatching	48
Life as a larva	50
Metamorphosis	52
Changes continue	54
Finishing touches	56
Enemies	58
Fascinating amphibians	60
Baby amphibians	62
Glossary	64
Index	65

Reptiles are made up of several groups, including turtles, tuataras, snakes, lizards, and crocodiles. Among many reptiles, rivalry among the males to court the females is usually violent. After mating takes place, many reptile females lay a large number of eggs. After incubation, the young emerge by breaking through the shell. Most of them must learn to manage on their own quickly, since few species can count on the protection of their parents.

The Reptiles

Finding a mate

There are about 6,770 kinds (or species) of reptiles. In many of them, the sexes differ in size, shape, or color. For example, male crocodiles are bigger than females. So are many male lizards. However, in some snakes and turtles it is just the opposite—the female is larger.

Like many other animals, reptiles reproduce only during certain times of the year. Reptiles have different ways of finding a mate. Some male snakes, for instance, find females of their species through smell. Male crocodiles roar to attract females.

Chuckawallas are large lizards that live in the desert. They lay 7–10 eggs at a time.

Male agamid lizards have bright colors on their head, crest, and throat. By making movements and getting into positions that show off these colors, they attract female agamids or announce to males of their species that they own the territory.

Sea turtles must lay their eggs on land. Some of them migrate thousands of miles to reach a beach where they nest.

The Nile crocodile lives in rivers and lakes in Africa. The male occupies a territory that includes some land on which he can bask in the sun. He patrols this territory from the water and chases off other male crocodiles. During the breeding season, the male roars to attract females to his territory, where he courts them and mates with them.

Fighting for the female

In reptiles, courtship and mating often take place in a territory that the male has set up. It usually includes places to hide, areas for basking in the sun, and food. When a male lizard sees an intruder in his territory, he will usually do a "threat display" before attacking. The intruder will do a threat display of his own. They will each try to look large and powerful by standing high on their legs, filling their lungs with air, and raising any crest of spiny scales on their head or back. At this point, a smaller, weaker male may back off and leave. Males who are more equal in size and strength may fight, but usually in a way that does not result in serious injury.

Male marine iguanas on the Galapagos Islands fight by butting their heads together, pushing and shoving each other. They also hit each other with their muscular tails, and if the fight becomes more violent, they bite.

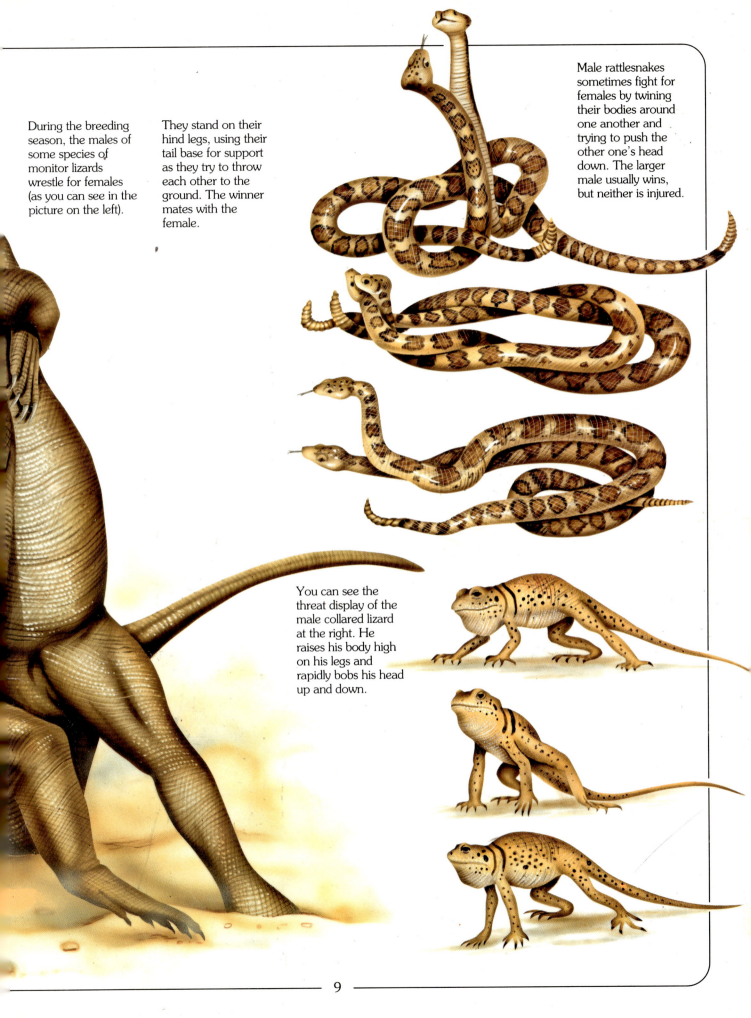

During the breeding season, the males of some species of monitor lizards wrestle for females (as you can see in the picture on the left).

They stand on their hind legs, using their tail base for support as they try to throw each other to the ground. The winner mates with the female.

Male rattlesnakes sometimes fight for females by twining their bodies around one another and trying to push the other one's head down. The larger male usually wins, but neither is injured.

You can see the threat display of the male collared lizard at the right. He raises his body high on his legs and rapidly bobs his head up and down.

Courtship and mating

It is important for animals to breed only with members of their own species. When two different species mate, the baby usually dies before birth or before it hatches. Courtship allows the male and female to find out that they belong to the same species and that they are adults who are ready to reproduce.

After he recognizes a female by her appearance or scent, a male will direct a series of movements or "displays" toward her. For example, while some male lizards bob their heads up and down, male alligators roar. The female recognizes the behavior of the male of her species, and if she is ready to reproduce, she will move toward him and allow him to mate with her.

During courtship, a male snake crawls over the female's body, placing his head over hers and trying to place his tail under or next to the female's tail.

During mating, which can last from 10 minutes to more than 24 hours, the male releases sperm into the cloaca of the female. These black ratsnakes are mating while hanging from a branch.

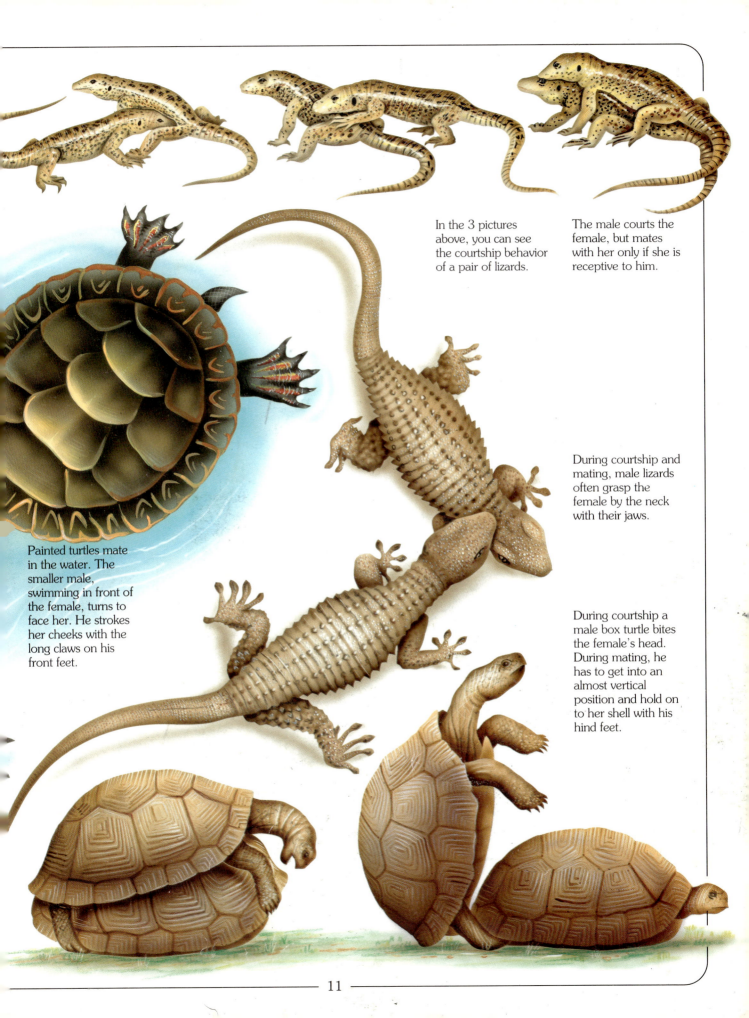

In the 3 pictures above, you can see the courtship behavior of a pair of lizards.

The male courts the female, but mates with her only if she is receptive to him.

During courtship and mating, male lizards often grasp the female by the neck with their jaws.

Painted turtles mate in the water. The smaller male, swimming in front of the female, turns to face her. He strokes her cheeks with the long claws on his front feet.

During courtship a male box turtle bites the female's head. During mating, he has to get into an almost vertical position and hold on to her shell with his hind feet.

Building a nest

After mating, most female reptiles lay their eggs in a protected spot, such as a hole in the ground, under logs or rocks, or under decaying plants. They build a nest that will hide the eggs from predators and other dangers, and provide the proper warmth and dampness needed for the eggs to develop and hatch.

Sea turtles, for example, nest on sandy beaches above the highest tide line, so that their eggs will not be flooded by sea water, which would kill them.

Coming ashore at night, the female sea turtle digs a shallow body pit slightly larger than she is to help her hide. She then uses her back flippers to dig a smaller hole in which she lays her eggs. She covers the nest with sand, leaving the eggs on their own, and returns to the sea. Just offshore, she will mate with a male. She may return to the same beach nest several more times during the mating season.

American alligators and some other crocodilians construct large nests out of plants and mud. Between 15 and 88 eggs at a time are laid by the American alligator, who will stay near the nest while the eggs incubate. Her presence will help keep predators away from the eggs.

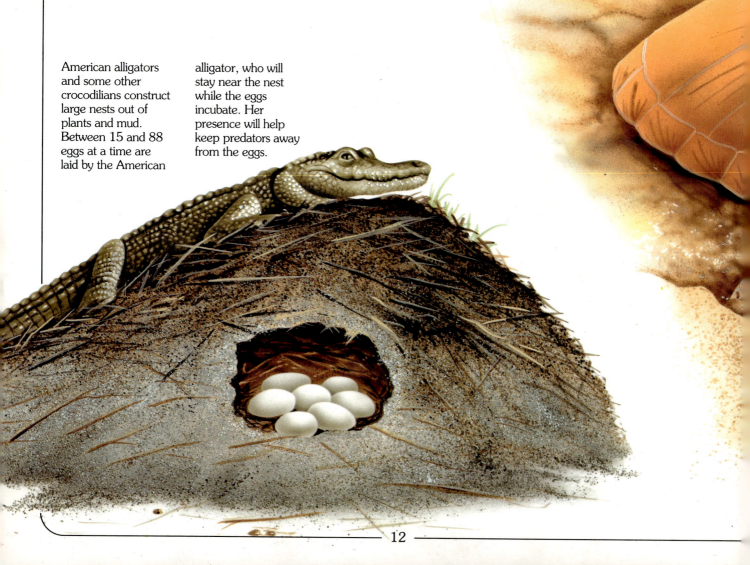

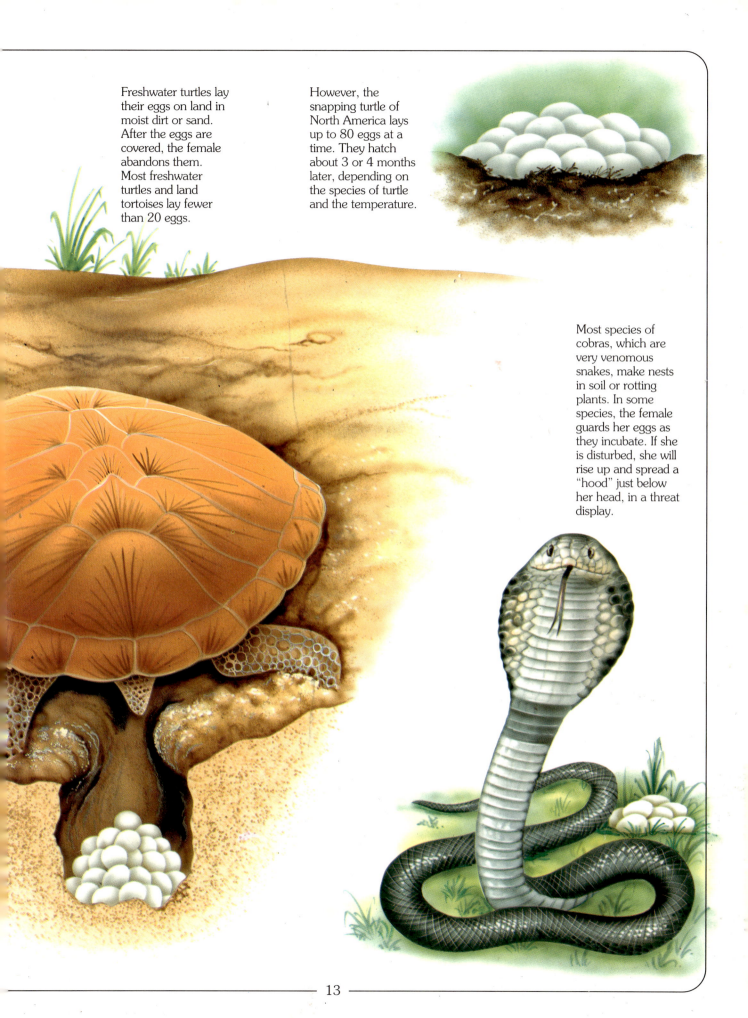

Freshwater turtles lay their eggs on land in moist dirt or sand. After the eggs are covered, the female abandons them. Most freshwater turtles and land tortoises lay fewer than 20 eggs.

However, the snapping turtle of North America lays up to 80 eggs at a time. They hatch about 3 or 4 months later, depending on the species of turtle and the temperature.

Most species of cobras, which are very venomous snakes, make nests in soil or rotting plants. In some species, the female guards her eggs as they incubate. If she is disturbed, she will rise up and spread a "hood" just below her head, in a threat display.

Reptile eggs

Reptiles were the first animals with backbones to lay eggs on dry land. Their eggs have a hard but porous shell that protects the embryo and at the same time lets it breathe. The embryo develops in the egg within membranes that are filled with fluid.

The baby hatches into a miniature version of its parents. It does not go through a "larval" stage, like a frog, which is a tadpole before it changes later into an adult frog.

Inside the shell, the reptile embryo is surrounded by the amnion, a sac of fluid that keeps it from drying out. The yolk sac provides food. The allantois forms a sac that stores the embryo's wastes, and is fused with the chorion, which lies against the shell. Blood vessels in the chorion carry oxygen, which the embryo needs to live, through the shell to the embryo.

ALLANTOIS

Snake eggs, like those on the left, are usually long and have a flexible, leathery shell.

Some reptiles care for their eggs as they develop. Some female skinks (a type of lizard) lick and turn their eggs. A female may even pick up an egg in her mouth and move it to a new position. She may gather up eggs that have been scattered from the nest and put them back in place.

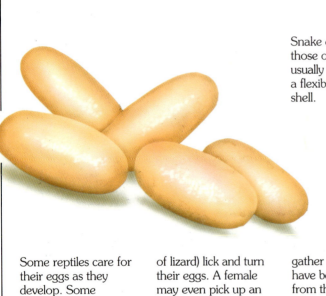

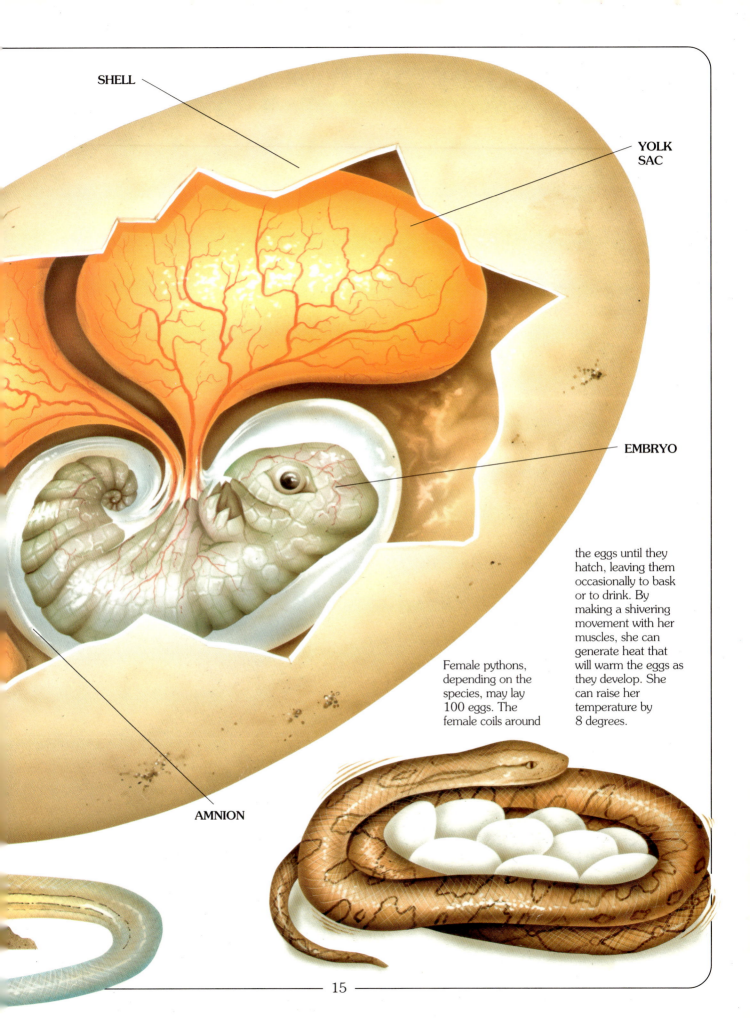

SHELL

YOLK SAC

EMBRYO

AMNION

Female pythons, depending on the species, may lay 100 eggs. The female coils around the eggs until they hatch, leaving them occasionally to bask or to drink. By making a shivering movement with her muscles, she can generate heat that will warm the eggs as they develop. She can raise her temperature by 8 degrees.

Reptiles that do not lay eggs

Most reptiles are oviparous, which means that they lay eggs. All turtles, alligators, crocodiles and their relatives, the tuataras, and most snakes and lizards lay eggs.

Some female lizards and snakes are ovoviviparous, which means they keep the eggs inside their bodies. Food for the embryo is provided by the yolk of the egg. Then, when the lizard or snake gives birth, the babies are fully developed and ready to live on their own.

There are a few viviparous lizards and snakes that not only keep the eggs in their bodies, but also provide food from the mother, as well as from the yolk sac. Their babies are also born fully developed and ready to live on their own.

Most sea snakes spend their entire lives in the oceans. They keep their eggs inside their body and give birth to live babies. They do not have to return to land to nest, the way sea turtles do.

The female asp viper on the left has given birth to live young. They are born surrounded by a membrane that breaks during labor, releasing the babies.

The slowworm, seen on the left, is a legless lizard that looks like a snake. It is ovoviviparous and gives birth to baby slowworms that are fully developed after about 3 months inside their mother's body.

One species of European smoothsnake is also ovoviviparous. It gives birth to live baby snakes, 3 to 15 at a time.

The lizard on the left is a type of skink that has very small limbs. It is ovoviviparous and gives birth to live babies, 3 to 13 at a time.

Development inside the egg

The yolk is the main source of food for the developing reptile embryo. It is contained in the yolk sac. In many reptiles, not all the yolk is used before hatching. The baby keeps the remaining yolk in its body after it hatches, and this yolk provides enough food for the first few days or weeks of its life. This helps the baby reptile survive while it learns to find or catch its food.

How long does it take for a reptile egg to hatch? That depends. Usually, eggs hatch 3 to 4 months after being laid. The eggs of the New Zealand tuataras—lizard-like reptiles—take 12 or 15 months to hatch!

Eggs absorb moisture from their environment as they develop. Many lizard and snake eggs have flexible, leathery shells that swell and become larger after they are laid.

During the last stages of its development as an embryo, a lizard's limbs form. At first, they look like paddles or webbed feet, but gradually they are transformed into feet with separate toes, covered with scales.

There are more than 550 species of iguanid lizards and many of them lay eggs. A small anolis lizard may lay one egg at a time, while a large common iguana can produce up to 71 eggs. These marine iguanas live only in the Galapagos Islands. They eat plants that grow in the ocean. Here they are basking in the sun to raise their body temperature before plunging into the cool waters of the ocean to feed.

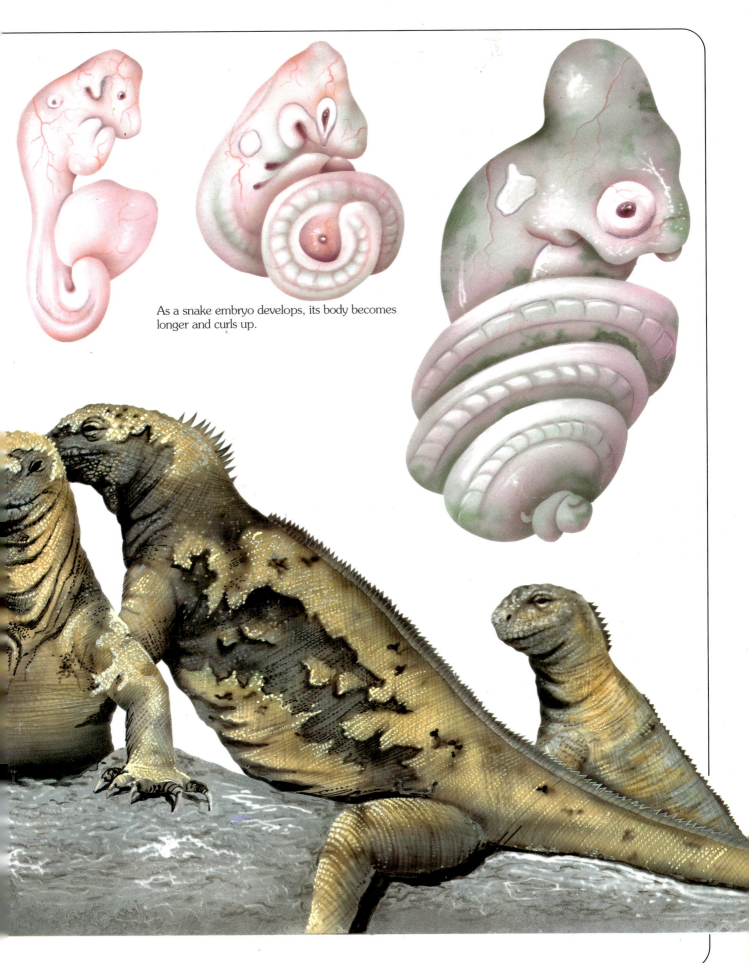

As a snake embryo develops, its body becomes longer and curls up.

Hatching

To help them escape from the egg when it is time to hatch, baby snakes have a sharp little tooth at the front of their mouth that they use to slice the eggshell open. Turtles, crocodiles, and their relatives have a hard bump at the end of their nose called an "egg caruncle," which they use to help them break out of the egg. Reptile parents that stay with their eggs during the incubation process sometimes help the babies to hatch.

This is how the eggs of the night lizard look when they are hatching.

Above, a python hatches. Using its egg tooth, it slits the shell and pushes its nose out for a look at the outside world. If disturbed, it may pull back into its shell, but it will eventually slide out.

Below, a gharial (a type of crocodilian) hatches. It is a small replica of its parents.

EGG TOOTH OF A HATCHING SNAKE

EGG CARUNCLE OF A HATCHING CROCODILE

EGG CARUNCLE OF A HATCHING TURTLE

Below, a tortoise hatches. Tortoise eggs usually have hard shells that crack open. Compare the tortoise egg here to the snake egg above.

Protecting the babies

Most reptiles do not care for their eggs or their young. Eggs are laid carefully in a place where they can incubate safely, but when babies hatch they are left on their own without help or protection from their parents. Most reptiles that give birth to live babies also abandon them.

The crocodilians—alligators, crocodiles, and their relatives—all take care of their eggs and their young. In many species the mother and sometimes the father remains at the nest during incubation. During hatching, the young make a squeaking noise that lets the adults know they are hatching. The adults then help the babies escape from the nest and carry them gently in their huge mouths to the water.

The Nile monitor lizard, above, may lay eggs in a termite mound, which protects them from predators and provides the right temperature and moisture levels.

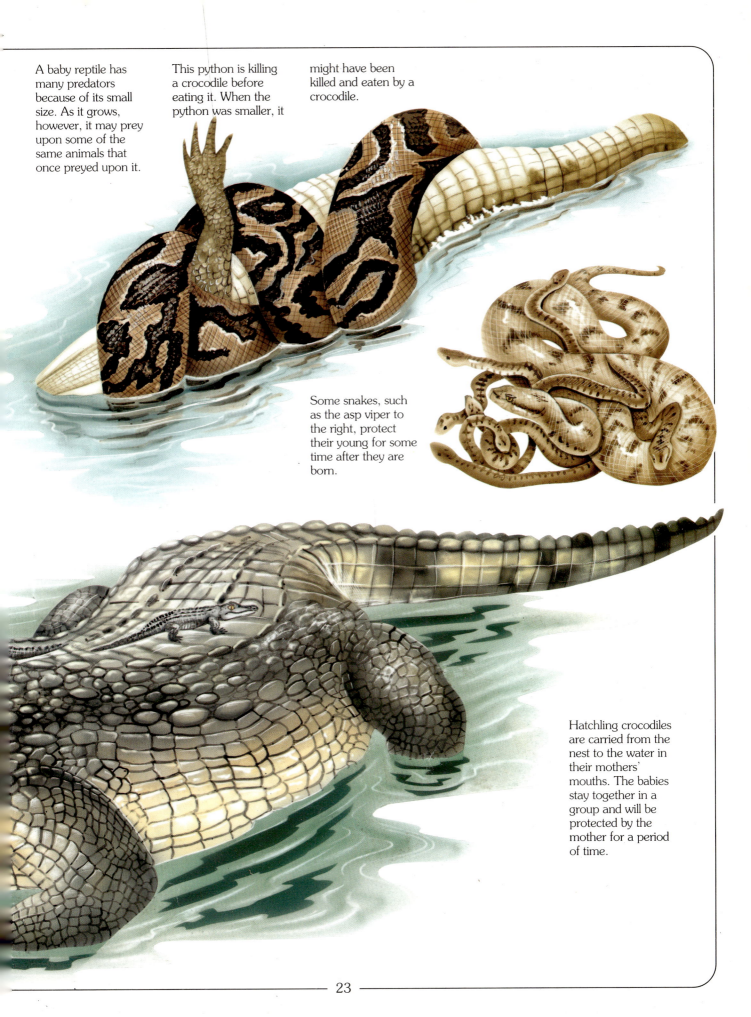

A baby reptile has many predators because of its small size. As it grows, however, it may prey upon some of the same animals that once preyed upon it.

This python is killing a crocodile before eating it. When the python was smaller, it might have been killed and eaten by a crocodile.

Some snakes, such as the asp viper to the right, protect their young for some time after they are born.

Hatchling crocodiles are carried from the nest to the water in their mothers' mouths. The babies stay together in a group and will be protected by the mother for a period of time.

Learning to live

Baby reptiles hatch or are born as miniature replicas of their parents. They are able to find food and survive on their own. Because they are small and relatively weak, there are many animals that would like to catch and eat them. As we have already seen, care by parents helps babies survive, but most must make it on their own.

Young reptiles are not known to play, the way young mammals do.

The toes of a climbing gecko's foot have adhesive pads that enable it to travel up and down vertical surfaces—even smooth ones, like glass—and walk upside down on ceilings.

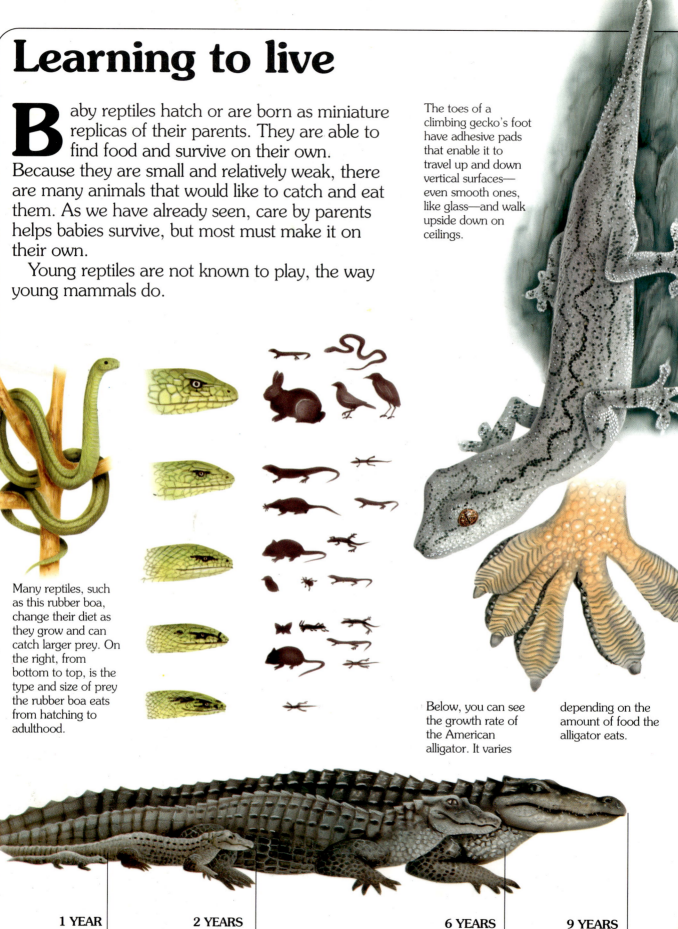

Many reptiles, such as this rubber boa, change their diet as they grow and can catch larger prey. On the right, from bottom to top, is the type and size of prey the rubber boa eats from hatching to adulthood.

Below, you can see the growth rate of the American alligator. It varies depending on the amount of food the alligator eats.

1 YEAR	2 YEARS	6 YEARS	9 YEARS
20 INCHES	40 INCHES	80 INCHES	100 INCHES
0.5 METRES	1 METRES	2 METRES	2.5 METRES

Monitor lizards, depending on the species, lay 7 to 37 eggs in a nest dug in the ground or in a termite nest. The mother abandons the eggs after she lays them and covers the nest. She will not care for the young after they hatch.

Sometimes, baby turtles do not leave the nest right away after they hatch. If the soil covering the nest has become dry and hard, they may have to wait for rain to soften it before they can break out.

Molting

Reptiles periodically shed the outer layer of their skin. Young reptiles shed more often than adults, and if the skin of a reptile is damaged, it will shed frequently until the damage is healed. Snakes shed their skin in one piece, while lizards usually shed their skin in patches.

Turtle scales, called scutes, fall off one at a time.

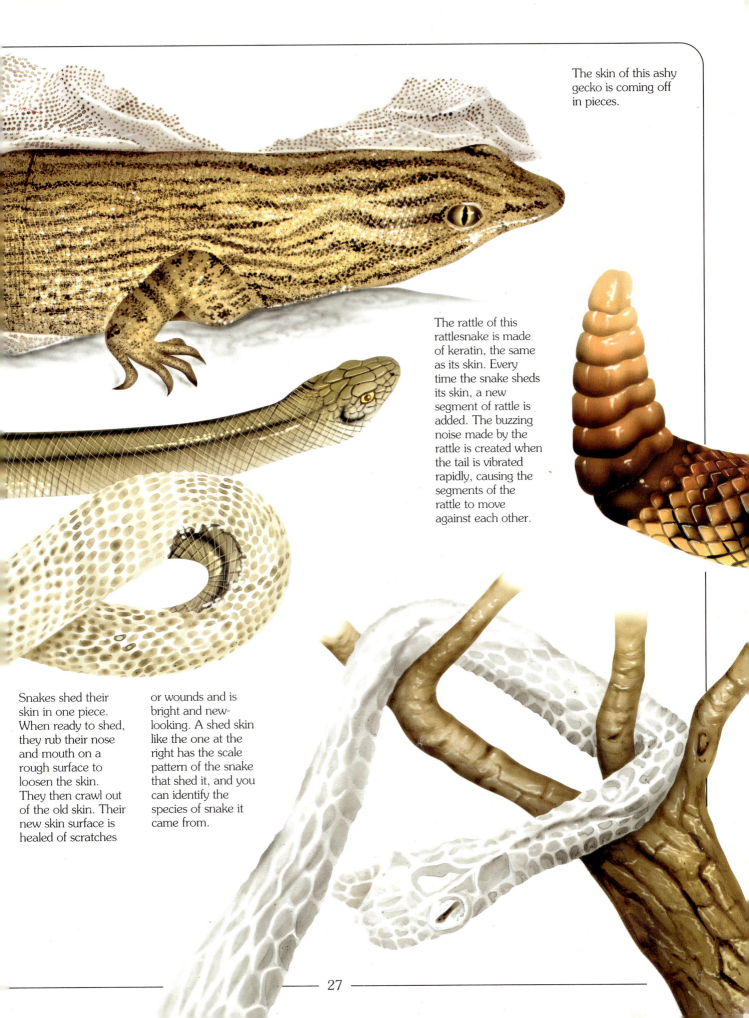

The skin of this ashy gecko is coming off in pieces.

The rattle of this rattlesnake is made of keratin, the same as its skin. Every time the snake sheds its skin, a new segment of rattle is added. The buzzing noise made by the rattle is created when the tail is vibrated rapidly, causing the segments of the rattle to move against each other.

Snakes shed their skin in one piece. When ready to shed, they rub their nose and mouth on a rough surface to loosen the skin. They then crawl out of the old skin. Their new skin surface is healed of scratches or wounds and is bright and new-looking. A shed skin like the one at the right has the scale pattern of the snake that shed it, and you can identify the species of snake it came from.

Escape from enemies

Babies of all animal species face many dangers and enemies when they are small. Baby reptiles, as we have seen, are no exception. Many are killed before they grow up. Adult reptiles also have predators. Birds, fish, mammals, and other reptiles all eat reptiles, and humans are the main predators of giant reptiles, such as crocodiles, tortoises, and pythons. In general, the larger the reptiles, the fewer predators they have.

Many reptiles are protected from predators by their color pattern, which camouflages them, and makes it difficult for predators to see them. This gecko looks like part of the tree trunk.

Some snakes eat other snakes, and may even eat the young of their own species.

Monitor lizards like to eat the eggs of crocodiles and will dig up and eat the eggs in unguarded nests.

The Dabb spiny-tailed lizard uses its thorny tail to block the mouth of the burrow in which it is hiding.

Many animals prey upon hatchling sea turtles as they leave the nest and run for the sea. Hungry birds and crabs catch them on the beach. Once they reach the sea, many will be eaten by fish and birds.

Fascinating reptiles

Most species of chameleons lay eggs.

The sandfish, a type of lizard known as a skink, lives in the desert. It "swims" just below the loose sand on the surface.

Small crocodiles have a color pattern that camouflages them, helping them to hide from the many animals that prey upon them.

Did you know that there is a "flying" lizard? Actually, it glides rather than flies. It lives in Southeast Asia and has large thin flaps of skin on its sides. When jumping from a perch, it unfolds its skin flaps and glides through the air.

The basilisk is a lizard the lives in parts of the American tropics. To escape its enemies, it sometimes runs across the surface of streams or rivers.

The thorny devil or Moloch is a lizard that lives in desert regions in Australia. Its spiny scales help protect it from being eaten by predators. The Moloch eats ants.

Giant tortoises, such as those found on the Galapagos Islands, have a very long life span. They may live as long as 150 years and weigh as much as 550 pounds (250kg).

The Australian frill-necked lizard has folds of skin around its neck. These large frills can be unfolded to make the lizard suddenly look much bigger than it really is.

Baby reptiles

The pattern on this baby staircase snake will change as it gets older. By the time it is an adult, the pattern will have disappeared.

This baby green mamba, a very poisonous snake even as a new hatchling, has just used its egg tooth to slice its way out of the egg.

The female Nile crocodile sometimes tosses one of her babies up in the air and catches it carefully in her mouth in order to transport it to safety.

Newly hatched iguanas must survive on their own without any help from their parents.

The tuataras—there are 2 species—are lizard-like reptiles that grow very slowly. It takes tuataras 11 to 13 years to reach the age at which they can reproduce.

The baby dwarf chameleon is very small, but shortly after birth it starts catching and eating small insects.

The fer-de-lance, a very poisonous snake found in the American tropics, gives birth to up to 70 young snakes. Even at birth these dangerous babies have fangs and venom.

Amphibians are a group of animals made up of many different species, including frogs, toads, newts, salamanders, and so on. Most amphibians are born and grow up by going through an amazing process called metamorphosis. The tadpole emerging from the egg does not resemble its parents in the slightest. It has no feet and does not have lungs. During the incredible adventure that is its life, it will gradually change its appearance until it looks like its parents and can live on land.

The Amphibians

Migrating to reproduce

More than 350 million years ago, the first amphibians came out of the water and colonized the land. Today there are more than 4,000 species of amphibians. They belong to 3 groups: 1) the frogs and toads, 2) the salamanders and newts, and 3) the caecilians.

Amphibians have not become totally independent of water, because most must return to fresh water to reproduce. They usually breed at the same time and place each year, and often in groups.

Most amphibians migrate from surrounding areas to ponds, lakes, or rivers to breed.

Toads, such as the one above, may crawl or hop slowly when migrating.

In some frog species, the male is smaller than the female. To the left you can see a female red eye tree frog carrying the smaller male on her back to the place where she will lay her eggs.

Not all amphibians go to ponds or lakes to reproduce. Some tropical frogs lay eggs inside epiphyites, plants whose leaves form a cup or reservoir that holds rainwater.

Attracting a mate

In North America and Europe, where the seasons change, frogs, toads, and salamanders migrate to breeding areas in the spring. Male frogs and toads usually get to the ponds and lakes before the females. Once there, they begin their mating calls. Each species of frog and toad has its own call that is made by the male and recognized by the female. This call helps the female to find a mate. The calls are often very loud.

Male salamanders do not have a mating call. The male crested triton at the right uses his bright colors and crest to attract the female, who recognizes him as a member of her species by his color pattern and body form.

Male frogs sometimes have fights over breeding territories, but seldom harm one another.

Hearing is an important sense for frogs because they communicate with sound. Here you can see the enormous eardrum of a frog, directly behind the eye.

Male frogs make their mating calls by moving air back and forth over their vocal cords between their inflated vocal pouches (you can see them under the frog's chin) and their lungs.

Vocal pouches vary in shape and position in different species of frog. For example, some frogs have 2 pouches, one on each side of the mouth. Others have one large pouch under the chin.

Courtship

When a female frog reaches a pond where males of her species are calling, she enters the water and swims up to the male whose call attracted her. He climbs on her back, wrapping his arms tightly around her, just behind her front feet. This is called amplexus and can last for several hours or even days. The picture of the frogs on page 41 shows frogs in amplexus.

Courtship in salamanders is different. The male salamander deposits a small packet of sperm called a spermatophore at the bottom of a pond or on the ground. He must guide the female to it and have her pick it up in her cloaca, the opening to her reproductive tract.

During the breeding season, some male frogs develop rough pads on their front feet to help them hold on to the slippery female.

The male alpine salamander rubs his chin along the female's back while scratching her skin with his teeth. This injects her with secretions produced in the glands under his chin. They make her more willing to mate.

Fertilization of the eggs takes place externally with this giant salamander. The female lays eggs in water and the male deposits his sperm on them.

The courtship of the crested triton takes place in the water. The male swims around the female, showing off his bright colors and the large crest on his back.

These frogs are in amplexus.

Laying the eggs

Most amphibians lay their eggs in water or in very damp places on land. Amphibian eggs lack a protective shell and dry out very quickly. This kills the egg.

A female frog in amplexus with a male carries him to the place where the eggs are to be laid. As she lays the eggs, the male fertilizes them.

Amphibian eggs are surrounded by a layer of protective jelly. The number of eggs produced varies with the species of amphibian. Some eggs are laid one at a time—separate from one another. Others are laid in long strings or in a big clump, touching one another.

Triturus salamanders lay eggs singly on the submerged leaves of water plants.

The grey tree frog of southern Africa breeds in groups in trees where it beats the eggs and seminal fluids with its feet, forming a foam nest.

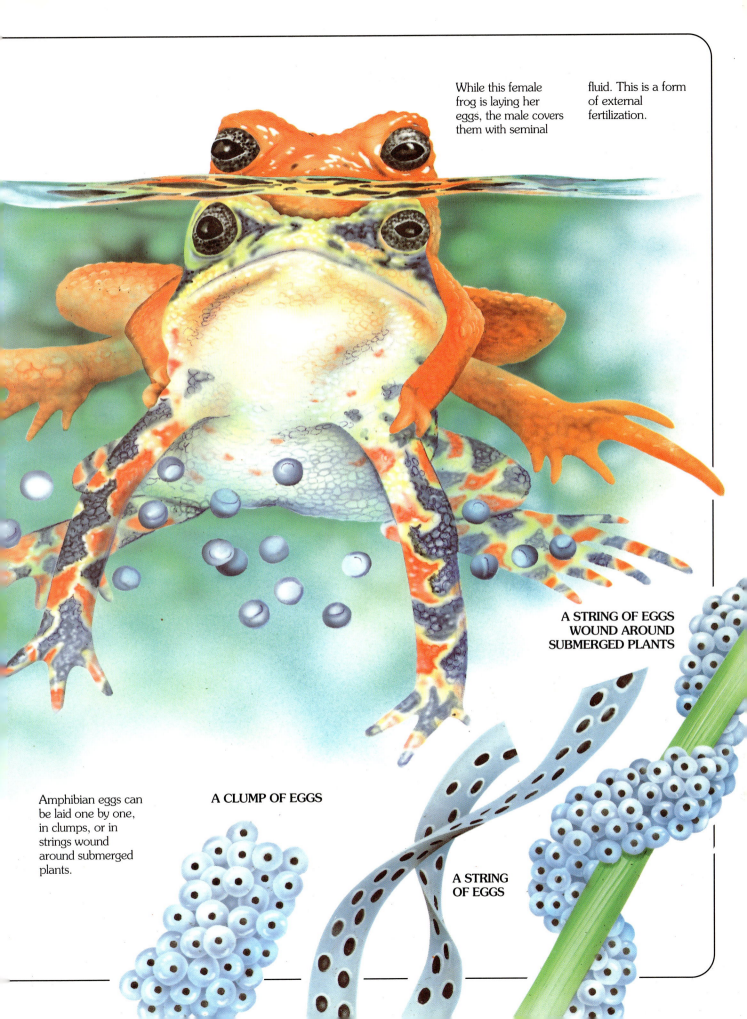

While this female frog is laying her eggs, the male covers them with seminal fluid. This is a form of external fertilization.

Amphibian eggs can be laid one by one, in clumps, or in strings wound around submerged plants.

A CLUMP OF EGGS

A STRING OF EGGS WOUND AROUND SUBMERGED PLANTS

A STRING OF EGGS

Eggs with special care

Most amphibians abandon their eggs after laying them, but a few species care for their eggs and their young. Amphibians that care for their eggs usually have many fewer eggs than those who abandon them.

Most amphibian eggs hatch into larvae—a form that does not resemble the adult at all—but eventually the larval forms change (or metamorphose) into adult amphibians. For example, most frog eggs hatch into tadpoles that look more like fish than frogs. Some species of frogs and salamanders lay eggs that develop directly into the adult form, without a larval stage.

A very few frogs keep their eggs inside their body after they are fertilized and while they develop. These species give birth to small frogs.

The male midwife toads of Europe and northern Africa carry their eggs on their back and thighs until they are ready to hatch and are taken to the water.

Some salamanders guard their eggs, which are laid in damp places on land, until they hatch.

The marsupial frog has a pouch in the skin on her back. She will carry her eggs in it until they are ready to hatch into tadpoles, at which time she will take them to the water.

Glass frogs lay their eggs on the leaves of plants overhanging streams. They stay with the eggs until they hatch. Then the tadpoles slide off the leaves and into the stream, where they will live in the water.

The brown salamander is shown above with her clutch of eggs.

Growing inside the egg

Food for amphibian embryos is provided by the yolk of the egg, just as it is for reptiles. The time it takes for amphibian eggs to hatch varies with the species and the temperature at which the eggs are kept. Some hatch in less than 24 hours, and others take several weeks.

Here you can see how a tree snake devours the eggs that a tropical frog had laid on a leaf, believing they would be safe.

Some frog eggs develop directly into baby frogs and do not have a tadpole stage. As you can see, the little frogs are already completely formed inside the eggs.

Females of the webbed-foot triton (a salamander) lay single eggs on submerged plants. A salamander egg that is laid in water hatches into a larval stage and lives in the water until it metamorphoses into an adult.

The black alpine salamander keeps its eggs in its body where they take 3 to 4 years to develop. When they are born, they resemble adults. There is no larval stage.

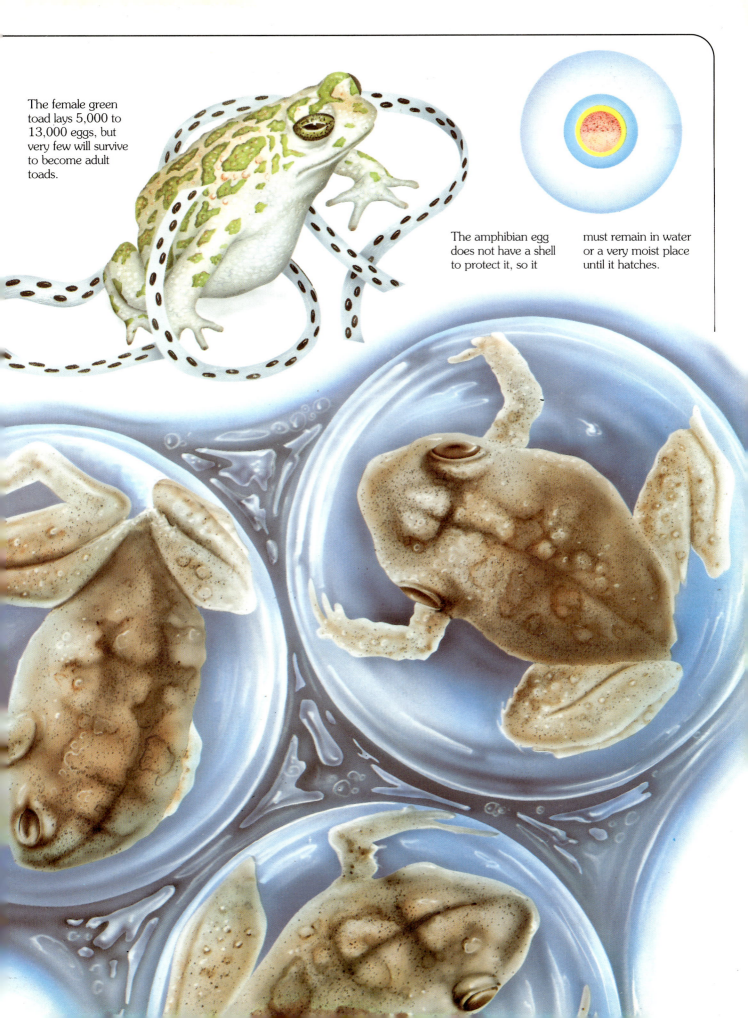

The female green toad lays 5,000 to 13,000 eggs, but very few will survive to become adult toads.

The amphibian egg does not have a shell to protect it, so it must remain in water or a very moist place until it hatches.

Hatching

Frog eggs usually hatch into tadpoles, the larval stage of frog development. Newly hatched tadpoles often do not swim away and begin feeding right away. They stay attached to the eggs they hatched from, hanging from the bottom of the egg mass.

The tadpoles breathe with gills located on either side of their head.

This poison dart frog guards her eggs (which were laid in a damp place on land) until they hatch. Then the tadpoles climb on her back and she carries them to the water, where they continue developing.

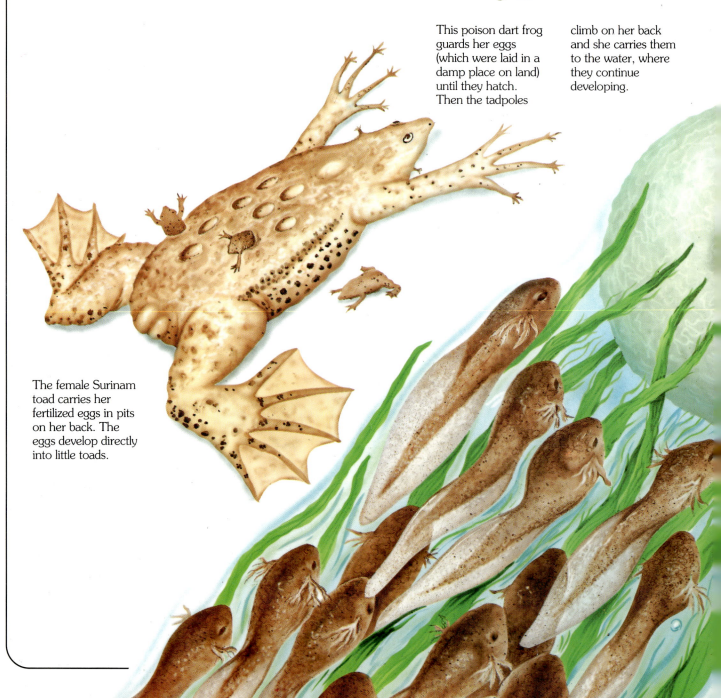

The female Surinam toad carries her fertilized eggs in pits on her back. The eggs develop directly into little toads.

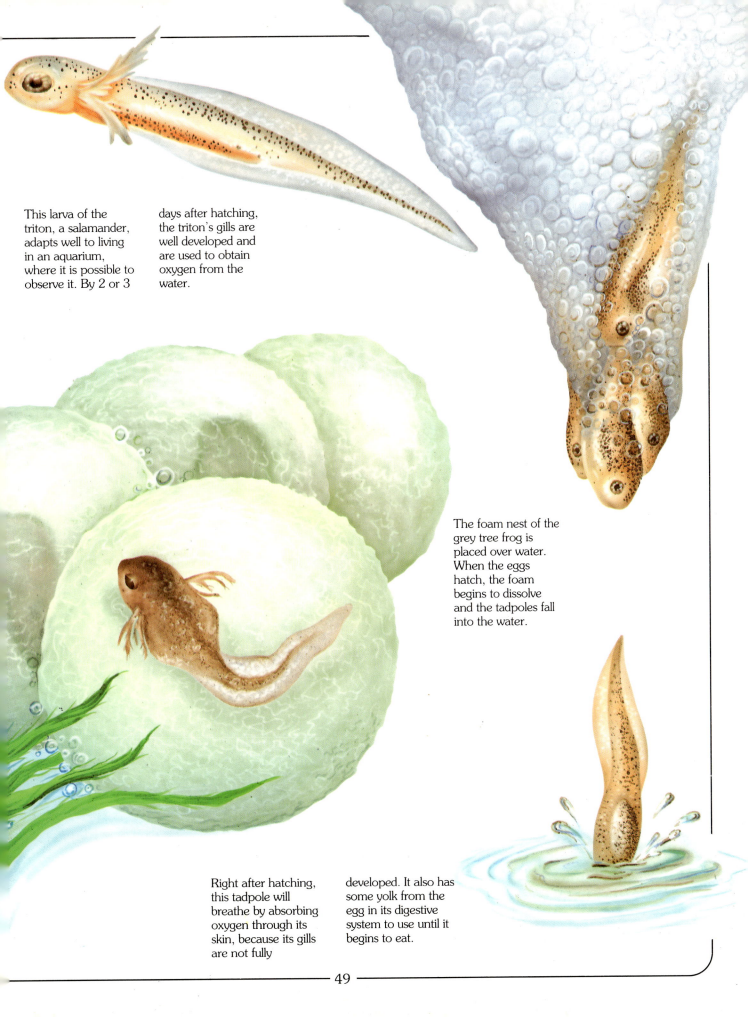

This larva of the triton, a salamander, adapts well to living in an aquarium, where it is possible to observe it. By 2 or 3 days after hatching, the triton's gills are well developed and are used to obtain oxygen from the water.

The foam nest of the grey tree frog is placed over water. When the eggs hatch, the foam begins to dissolve and the tadpoles fall into the water.

Right after hatching, this tadpole will breathe by absorbing oxygen through its skin, because its gills are not fully developed. It also has some yolk from the egg in its digestive system to use until it begins to eat.

Life as a larva

Tadpoles that hatch from eggs laid in water will live in the water until they change into adult frogs. They swim using their tails and breathe using their gills. Most of them eat plants, using mouth parts with rows of small teeth.

There are many different types of tadpoles that have different kinds of anatomy, lifestyles, and ways of feeding. They also take different lengths of time to develop—depending on the species.

The male Trinidad frog carries his tadpoles to a stream where they will live until their metamorphosis into baby frogs.

Sometimes tadpoles die when the pond they are living in dries up.

If you look closely, you will see that the tadpole is similar to a fish. Both have tails and breathe with gills. Most frog tadpoles eat algae (plants) rather than animals.

Tadpoles usually eat vegetable matter, but often will eat dead animals, including dead tadpoles that they find.

The male Darwin frog picks up hatchling tadpoles and carries them in his vocal sac. They hop out of his mouth as little frogs!

Metamorphosis

After spending time as larvae, amphibians change their body form to resemble the adults of their species. Frog tadpoles (larvae) have fat, round bodies and mouth parts designed to scrape vegetable matter from water plants and algae. They breathe with gills and cannot live on land.

During metamorphosis, they change their body form completely, as you can see in the pictures to the right. They also change from animals that eat plants to animals that catch and eat other animals.

THE METAMORPHOSIS OF A FROG

1. The egg

2. The embryo ready to come out

3. About 3 days after hatching, the external gills start to work (they look almost like feathers), and the tadpole starts to eat algae

4. At 3 weeks old, the tadpole takes in water mouth. It passes over gills, formed about 6 da after hatching, and is forced out through a ho in the skin.

Caecilians are legless, burrowing amphibians. They normally live in tropical areas, underground or in water. Some lay eggs that hatch into larvae and later metamorphose into the adult form. Others give birth to living young that developed inside the mother's body without a larval stage.

The greater siren is a large salamander that can reach a length of 3 feet (90cm). It lives in water as an adult and resembles the larval stage of other salamanders.

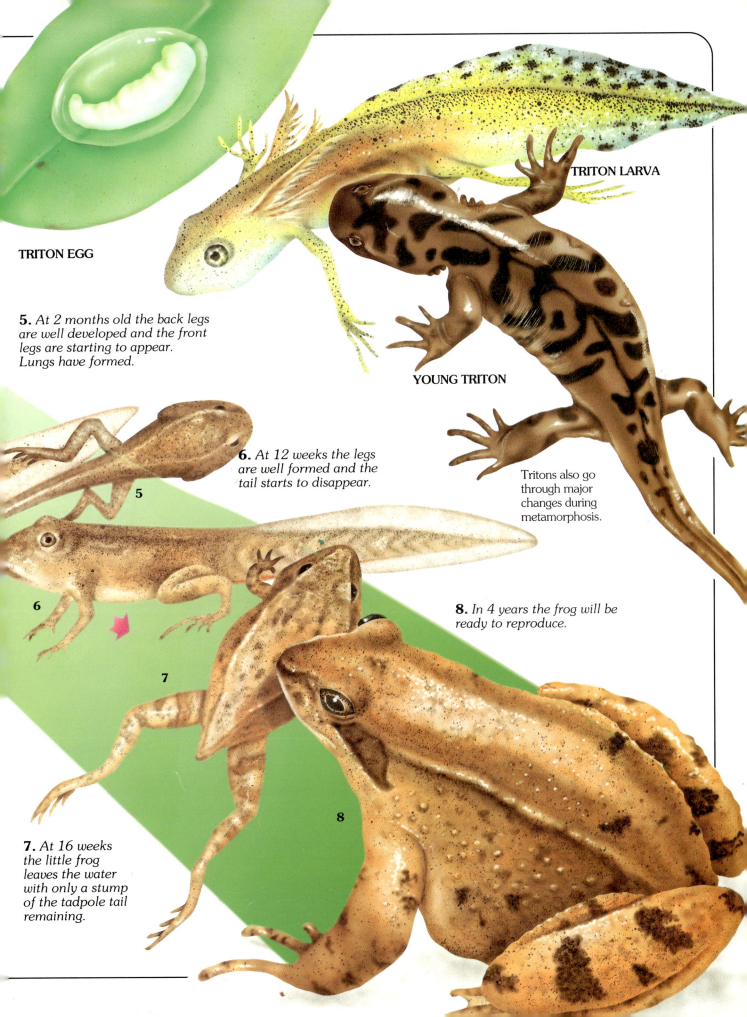

TRITON EGG

TRITON LARVA

YOUNG TRITON

5. *At 2 months old the back legs are well developed and the front legs are starting to appear. Lungs have formed.*

6. *At 12 weeks the legs are well formed and the tail starts to disappear.*

Tritons also go through major changes during metamorphosis.

8. *In 4 years the frog will be ready to reproduce.*

7. *At 16 weeks the little frog leaves the water with only a stump of the tadpole tail remaining.*

Changes continue

You can see, in the pictures of the frog tadpoles to the right, that as the tadpole gets older and its legs grow, it begins to look like a frog. The head of the frog can be seen; the eyes are larger, and the general shape is more frog-like.

Salamanders look more like primitive amphibians than any other types do. Except for their gills, larval salamanders usually look like their parents. They have 4 legs and a tail that are in about the same place as they are in the adult. Compare them to the frog larvae.

Tadpole at 4 weeks

Tadpole at 2 months

Tadpole at 3 months

THREE PHASES IN GROWTH OF A TADPOLE

As the tail muscles become stronger and the caudal fin increases in size, the tadpoles are ready to swim with more force. Later on, the back legs become better developed and help the tadpole swim.

The shape of the feet and toes of amphibians gives clues to the lifestyle of the animals.

Frogs that live in trees have adhesive toe pads.

Spines on males' front feet grip females during mating.

Frogs that live in water usually have webbed feet to aid in swimming.

The foot of a land-dwelling salamander

"Flying" frogs use their webbed feet to help them glide when they jump from one perch to another.

Finishing touches

As the tadpole becomes a frog, its mouth changes position and becomes much larger. Soon it will catch insects and eat them. The larger tadpoles are no longer easy prey for enemies like dragonfly larvae. They can breathe through both their skin and their lungs.

When the tadpole is 12 weeks old, only the stump of the tail is left and the young frogs leave the water to live and breathe on land. They will stay close to the water for some time.

During metamorphosis the back legs grow and become strong in preparation for leaping, the adult frog's way of moving.

This tree frog has metamorphosed and left the water, but it still has some of its tail left.

As the lungs develop, the metamorphosing frog spends more and more time breathing air.

Some frogs with poisonous skin have bright colors to warn predators away. The warning colors develop as the tadpole grows.

Amphibians have skin that allows water to pass through it very easily. Their skin has glands that secrete mucus, sticky stuff that slows down the loss of water through the skin.

Enemies

Not all tadpoles get to become adults. Most will be eaten by other animals. Many animals like to eat amphibian larvae—birds, mammals, reptiles, insects, and even other amphibians. The tadpoles are an important food source for these other animals, allowing them to live, grow, reproduce, and feed their young.

Many fish eat tadpoles as part of their regular diet.

Most frogs eat insects after they metamorphose.

Dragonflies are now the frog's prey, rather than the tadpole's predators.

Birds are important predators of amphibians—both larval and adult.

Dragonfly nymphs frequently eat tadpoles, capturing them with their powerful jaws.

This toad is hard to see among the water plants. It is well camouflaged.

Poison dart frogs, found in the American tropics, are small. The largest of them are only 2½ inches (6.3cm) long. They are active during the day, hunting for ants and other small insects on the forest floor. They have very toxic skin, which helps protect them from predators.

Fascinating amphibians

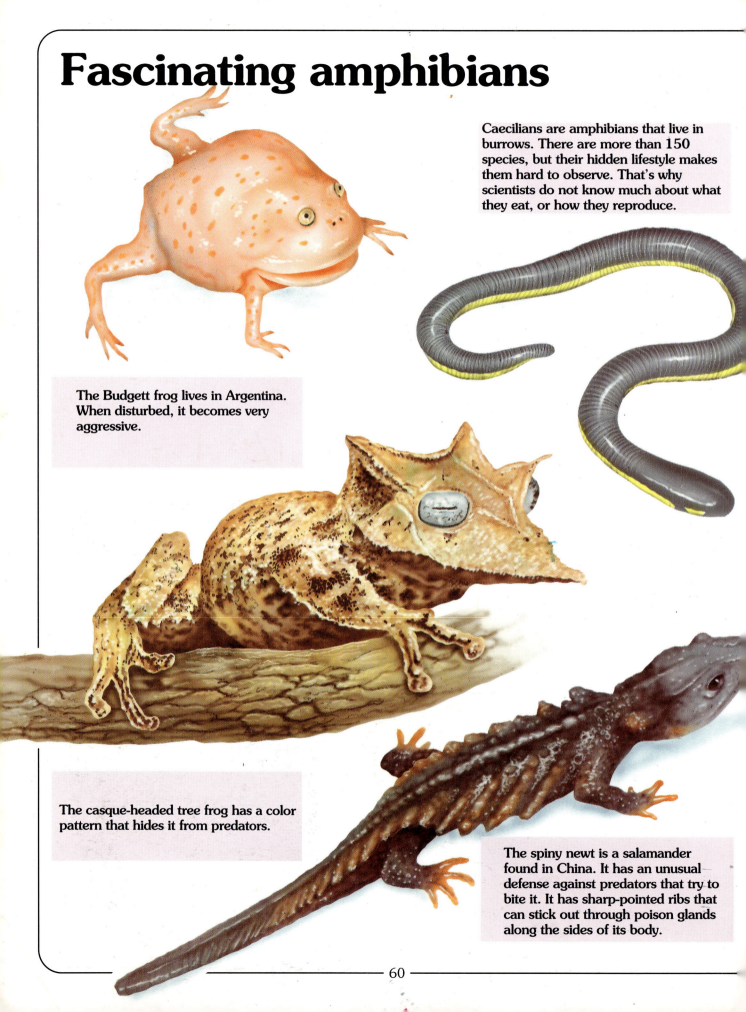

Caecilians are amphibians that live in burrows. There are more than 150 species, but their hidden lifestyle makes them hard to observe. That's why scientists do not know much about what they eat, or how they reproduce.

The Budgett frog lives in Argentina. When disturbed, it becomes very aggressive.

The casque-headed tree frog has a color pattern that hides it from predators.

The spiny newt is a salamander found in China. It has an unusual defense against predators that try to bite it. It has sharp-pointed ribs that can stick out through poison glands along the sides of its body.

The olm salamander lives in caves in Europe. It looks like a larva, which it is. It does not metamorphose, but unlike other amphibian larvae, it can reproduce.

The axolotl, another salamander that remains in the larval stage as an adult, lives in water. Most are grey, but some, like the one pictured here, are albino, and are white.

The bright skin color of this poison dart frog warns frog predators of its very toxic skin. Biting this frog will make a predator very sick very quickly. The next time it sees a poison dart frog, it will probably leave it alone. This frog is shown many times life size.

Baby amphibians

While the larvae of frogs do not look at all like their parents, the larvae of salamanders do.

This South American marsupial frog has her pouch on her back, and it is filled with developing eggs. When they hatch, she will go to the water and release the tadpoles. They will continue to develop away from their mother.

The tadpole of the paradox frog grows to be almost 4 times larger than the adult frog. Most frogs become larger than they were as tadpoles, not the reverse!

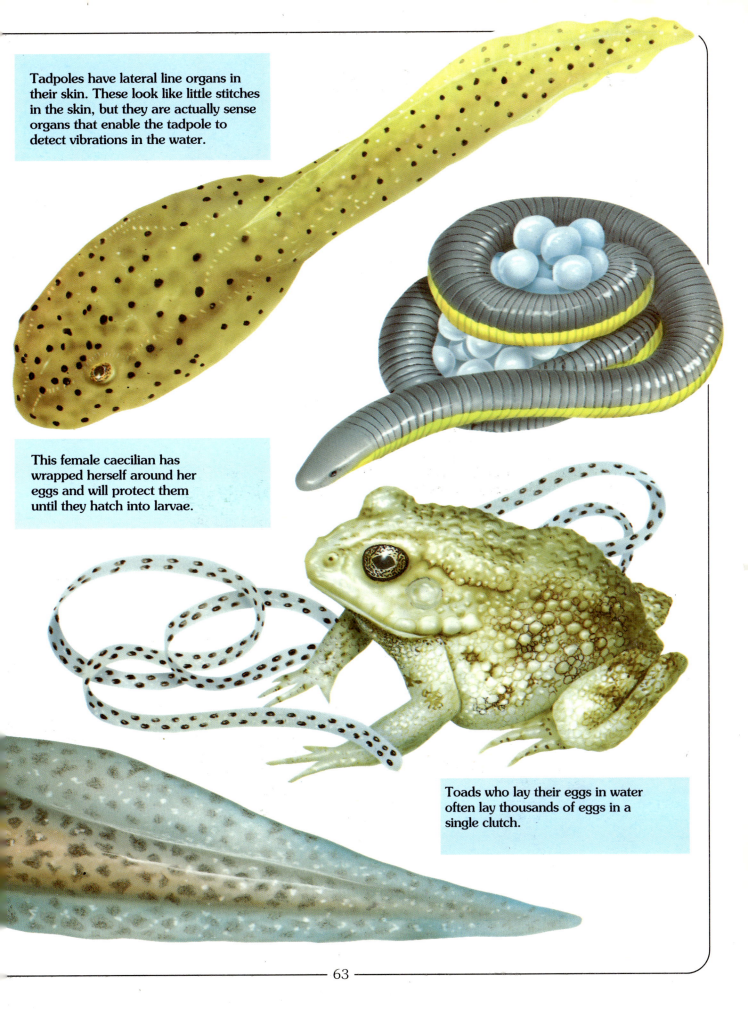

Tadpoles have lateral line organs in their skin. These look like little stitches in the skin, but they are actually sense organs that enable the tadpole to detect vibrations in the water.

This female caecilian has wrapped herself around her eggs and will protect them until they hatch into larvae.

Toads who lay their eggs in water often lay thousands of eggs in a single clutch.

Glossary

Cloaca. The opening at the tail end of the body of reptiles, where waste products from the kidneys and intestines are eliminated. The reproductive tract also opens into the cloaca. Eggs are laid and young born through the cloaca. Sperm is introduced into the female's cloaca during mating.

Clutch. The eggs laid by a female during a single breeding event. During the breeding season, a lizard might lay a clutch of 4 eggs 3 times. Each group of eggs laid together is a clutch.

Embryo. The young of an animal before it hatches from an egg or is born to live independently of its mother.

Fertilization. The moment when a sperm from a male animal unites with the egg of a female animal.

Hatch. An egg hatches when the embryo has completed development and is ready to live outside the egg.

Incubation. A method of providing eggs with proper conditions of temperature and moisture so that the embryos can develop and hatch.

Larva. The stage of development of an animal after it hatches from an egg but is not yet in the adult form and usually cannot reproduce. Most amphibian eggs hatch into larvae that will metamorphose or change into an adult frog, salamander, or caecilian. Reptile eggs hatch into a small version of the adult reptile that produced them.

Mating. The process in which the male inserts his penis or hemipenis into the cloaca of a female in order to transfer sperm into the female's body. The sperm enter the female's reproductive tract and eventually fertilize her eggs.

Molting. The periodic shedding of skin or feathers that occurs in all animals.

Oviparous. A term used to refer to animals that reproduce by laying eggs.

Ovoviviparous. A term used to refer to animals that retain their eggs in their bodies during development, and that give birth to live young. Food for the developing embryo is provided by the yolk of the egg.

Predator. An animal that catches and eats other animals.

Scales. The outer layers of the skin of reptiles forms small hard plates called scales. They can have many shapes and sizes.

Seminal fluid. Fluid produced by the male, which contains the sperm. It is placed by the male into the cloaca of the female or spread over eggs the female has laid.

Sperm. The sex cells from the male animal that unite with the egg produced by the female.

Viviparous. A term used to refer to animals in which embryonic development of the egg takes place within the mother. The mother also provides food for the embryo through a connection between her circulatory system and the embryos.

Index

Agamid lizards, 6
Albinos, 61
Allantois, 14
Alligators, 12, 24
American alligators, 12, 24
Amnion, 14
Amplexus, 40-41, 42
Anolis lizard, 18
Asp viper, 16, 23
Australian frill-necked
    lizard, 31
Axolotl, 61
Baby, 28; reptiles, 14-25,
    28-29, 32-33;
    amphibians, 62-63
Basilisk, 31
Boa, rubber, 24
Budgett frog, 60
Caecilians, 52, 60, 63
Camouflage, 27, 30
Caruncle, egg, 20-21
Casque-headed tree frog, 60
Chameleons, 30, 33
Chorion, 14
Chuckwallas, 7
Cobra, 13
Collared lizard, 9
Courtship, reptile, 6-11;
    amphibians, 38-41
Crested triton, 38
Crocodiles, 6-7, 21-23,
    30, 32
Dabb spiny-tailed lizard, 29
Darwin frog, 51
Displays, see Threat display
Dragonflies, 58, 59
Eggs, reptile, 14-15, 18-19,
    22; snake, 14;
    amphibian, 42-49
Embryo, 14-15, 18-19
Enemies, 28-29;
    amphibians, 58-59
Epiphites, 37
Fer-de-lance, 33
Fighting: reptiles, 8-9;
    amphibians, 38
Flying lizard, 30
Frogs, 37, 38-45, 47-63
Galapagos Islands, 8, 18, 31
Gecko, 27, 28
Gharial, 21
Hatching, reptile, 20-21;
    amphibian, 48-49
Hearing, 38
Iguanas, 8, 18, 33
Iguanid lizards, 18
Keratin, 27
Larvae, 50-55, 58, 61-62
Lizards, 6, 8-11, 22, 25, 29,
    30-31
Mamba, green, 32
Marsupial frog, 45, 62
Mating, reptile, 6-11;
    amphibians, 38-39
Metamorphosis, 52-57
Migration, amphibian, 36-37
Moloch, 31
Molting, 26-27
Monitor lizards, 9, 22, 25, 29
Mucus, 57
Nest, building a, 12-13
Newt, spiny, 60
Night lizard, 20
Nile: crocodile, 7, 32;
    monitor lizard, 22
Olm, 61
Oviparous reptiles, 16
Ovoviviparous reptiles, 16
Paradox frog, 62
Poison dart frog, 48, 59
Python: hatching, 19;
    killing crocodile, 23
Rattlesnakes, 9, 27
Salamanders, 38, 40-42, 45-
    46, 49, 52-55, 60-61
Sandfish, 30
Scales, turtle, 26
Scutes, 26
Siren, 52
Skin, shedding, 26-27
Skinks, 14, 17, 30
Snakes, 6, 10, 12, 15-17,
    19-21, 23-24, 26-28,
    32-33, 46; eggs, 14-15;
    sea, 16; smooth, 17;
    tree, 46
Staircase snake, 32
Surinam toad, 48
Tadpoles, 50-58, 62-63
Temperature, snake, 15
Territory, 6-8
Thorny devil, 31
Threat display, 8-10
Toads, 36, 38, 47, 59, 63
Tortoise, 21, 31; giant, 31;
    land, 13
Trinidad frog, 50
Triton, 49, 53; crested, 38,
    41; webbed-foot, 46
Triturus salamanders, 42
Tuaturas, 18, 33
Turtles, 6, 21; baby, 25;
    box, 11; fresh water, 13;
    painted, 11; scales, 26;
    sea, 12, 29;
    snapping, 13, 25-26, 29
Viviparous lizards and
    snakes, 16
Worm, slow, 17
Yolk, 14-15, 16, 18, 46
Young, caring for, 22-23; live,
    16-17; survival of,
    24-25, 28-29